MW01710804

The Complete Plays

of

William Shakespeare

OTHER WORKS BY ERIC KIM

(with J. Torres)

Love as a Foreign Language Vol. 1 & 2
Degrassi Extra Credit: Vol. 3: Missing You

(webcomics)

Battle Academy
Streta

(upcoming)

Future Imperfect
Billy Smoke

The Complete Plays of William Shakespeare

As Adapted by Eric Kim

INKSKRATCH PUBLISHING TORONTO

Dedication

To my friends
And the retarded things that make us laugh
This one's for all of you

Edited by Andrew Wheeler, Derek Halliday
Art direction and book design by Eric Kim

© 2010 by Eric Kim

All rights reserved. No part of this book may be reproduced without written permission from the publisher, except by a reviewer who may quote brief passages or reproduce illustrations in a review with appropriate credits; nor many any part of this book be reproduced, stored in a retrieval system, or transmitted in any form or by any means — electronic, mechanical, photocopying, recording, or other — without written permission from the publisher.

Inkskratch books are available for special premium and promotional uses and for customized editions. For further information, please contact us at eek@inkskratch.com.

Inkskratch Publishing
592 Markham St.
Toronto, ON, M6G 2L8
www.inkskratch.com

Printed in Canada

Library and Archives Canada Cataloguing in Publication
Kim, Eric
The Complete Plays of William Shakespeare adapted by Eric Kim / Eric Kim
ISBN 978-0-9865747-0-2
1. Humour / General. 2. Comics.

A Catalogue

Of the overall Comedies Histories & Tragedies contained in this volume

COMEDIES

HISTORIES

HISTORIES (con't)

TRAGEDIES

A Short Introduction

The works of Shakespeare have always been subject to wide-ranging reinterpretation. In the early 19th century, Charles and Mary Lamb revised Shakespeare's plays as children's stories. Around the same time, Thomas Bowdler produced editions of the plays that omitted any words or phrases deemed inappropriate to a family audience. Since that time, the plays have often taken on new colours in performance, from post-Colonial adaptations of *The Tempest*, to versions of *The Merchant of Venice* that recast Shylock as the sympathetic hero, to the striking reinvention of the Scottish play as a Japanese movie.

Of course, none of this can be taken as licence for the terrible literary debasements collected in this book. As the following pages will reveal, Eric Kim has merrily taken his scrivening tools to the Bard's great works like a sugar-crazed child attacking a piñata. By taking the grace, complexity, beauty and ambiguity of Shakespeare's words and reducing them down to vulgar two-panel cartoons, he has first danced on the poet's grave, and then urinated freely on the headstone. The book you hold in your hands is an *abomination.*

Such is the depth of Kim's contempt for Shakespeare's work that he only asked me to write the introduction because I'm the only Englishman he knows. Eric assumes that every Englishman spends his formative years hip-deep in sonnets and soliloquies, learning the words to *Henry V*'s celebrated St Crispin's Day speech and devising theoretical adaptations of *A Midsummer Night's Dream.*

Frustratingly, in my case, this is all absolutely true. I do know a thing or two about the Bard of Avon. Above all else, I know that he's resilient, and he's survived far worse than Eric Kim can throw at him. He even survived a version of *Twelfth Night* starring Amanda Bynes and Channing Tatum. He'll get through this. Indulge this latest hack work with a clean conscience, dear reader; they haven't buried Shakespeare yet.

Besides, it is quite funny.

~ Andrew Wheeler, Toronto, February 2010

-- WE'D LIKE YOU TO GIVE A WARM WELCOME TO A BUDDING YOUNG PLAYWRIGHT AND STANDUP COMIC, WILLY SHAKESPEARE
THIS GUY SUCKS
HIC

AAAAAAAAH--!
SNF! MOMMY! BABY BOY ISN'T CRYING MOMMY! SNIF
ES
UK
OOOH BOY. THIS IS AWKWARD.
I DON'T THINK THIS ONE'S GONNA MAKE IT.
C. MARLOWE
T. KYD

THE TEMPEST.

Score: 0 of 250
Esc = Help
You are on a magic island.
A storm has seperated you from your party.
A girl named MIRANDA stands before you. She says her dad is a magician.
IT'S A MAN!
HEE HEE
A. Tell her she's on drugs.
B. Say "hello" and prove your love by doing chores.
C. Drink the Water of Life & look into that place the B.G. fear.
D. Take a moment to stare at all the weird shit around you.

Score: 249 of 250
Esc=Help
The magician is Prospero, former Duke of Milan! He's gotten his Dukedom back from his brother Antonio, the usurper.
I'll keep your plot to kill the King a secret. Thanks for the returning my title!
Go fuck yourself!
A. Stay with the odd, Björkish girl, Miranda.
B. Go to Milan! Why are you still here?!
C. Get wasted with Caliban, the frecked monster.
D. A & C, but not B. This place is too fun.

TWO GENTLEMEN OF VERONA

GASP! MY SERVANT IS ACTUALLY MY FIANCÉE IN DISGUISE! WHAT HAVE I DONE?!
UH... IT'S OKAY, DUDE. NOW STEP AWAY FROM ME AND MY GIRLFRIEND.
THERE'S NO WAY THAT'S GONNA WORK OUT. NUH-UH.
I HAVE FAINTED

MERRY WIVES OF WINDSOR

OH MISTRESS FORD, WE'VE HAD SUCH AMUSEMENTS AT FALSTAFF'S EXPENSE!
INDEED! NOW LET US SEE IF WE CAN MANIPULATE THOSE TWO LADS IN WEDDING ONE ANOTHER!

MEASURE FOR MEASURE

BALLS. YOU ARE THE DUKE!
LIVE & LEARN, KID. OBSERVE!
ISABELLE, I SAVED YOUR BROTHER. NOW LET'S GET HITCHED AND BUMP UGLIES.
...I WAS GONNA BE A NUN BEFORE I MET YOU ASSHOLES.

THE COMEDY OF ERRORS

ARGUE
HOT DOG
ANGRY
BICKER
SWEAR
SPIT!
WORDS
HISS!
CURSE
FIGHT
...IN HINDSIGHT, WE PROBABLY SHOULD HAVE BEEN MORE CREATIVE WITH THE NAMES.
AGREED, MA.

MUCH ADO ABOUT NOTHING

I SHOULDN'T HAVE LISTENED TO THE HYPE--
WAIT. YOU'RE ALIVE??
HA! FAKED YOU OUT. LET'S GET MARRIED!
SURPRISE! I DO LOVE MOVIES. LET'S GET MARRIED!
THAT'S LOGICAL. LET'S!
SPROING

LOVE'S LABOUR LOST

3 YEARS LATER...
WELL, WE DID IT! NOW LET'S GET IT ON!
UM... THE KING DIED. SO WE GOTTA GO...
WHY DON'T YOU PROVE YOUR LOVE TO US IN THE MEANTIME?
HOW?
YOU'VE GOT A YEAR AND A DAY TO FIGURE IT OUT. LATER!
FWUMP
SASHAY
SAUNTER

A MIDSUMMER NIGHT'S DREAM

WHOA! I'M NOT A DONKEY NO MORE!
YEAH, YOU ARE!

THE MERCHANT OF VENICE

≡SIGH≡ OKAY, HE'S DEFAULTING. SO YOU CAN HAVE THE FLESH, BUT NO BLOOD.
CAN'T SPILL THE BLOOD OF CHRISTIANS, EVIL JEW!
...AND YOU ALSO GOTTA GIVE UP YOUR CASH AND CONVERT THANKS TO OUR TRUMPED-UP CONSPIRACY CHARGE!
I BELIEVE I'M BEING PROFILED

AS YOU LIKE IT

... AND IT ALL WORKS OUT WITH EVERYONE GETTING MARRIED.
UH... WE HAD MORE EXPOSITION...

THE TAMING OF THE SHREW

COME HITHER, WIFE!
I OBEY
CAN YOU BELIEVE THAT SHIT??
I DUNNO, BUT NOW I THINK YOUR SISTER'S HOT.

ALL'S WELL THAT ENDS WELL

LATER!
BABY
THIS BITCH IS NUCKIN' FUTS.
I LOVE YOU, BABY.
VIVA ITALIA

TWELFTH NIGHT

AW DUDE, I TOTALLY PLAYED YOU. I'M A CHICK!
I'M SUCH A STALKER
I'M OVER IT.

THE WINTER'S TALE

16 YEARS LATER
MAN. I TOTALLY SHOULDN'T HAVE PULLED THAT SHIT 16 YEARS AGO!
HI! I'M THE DAUGHTER OF THE EXILED QUEEN. I'M MARRYING THE PRINCE OF BOHEMIA!
HERE WE GO AGAIN

KING RICHARD II NEVER TOLD YOU WHAT HAPPENED TO YOUR FATHER.
HE TOL ME EN HE T ME YOU KILLED HIM!
NO. I AM YOUR FATHER.
HGOD OHGOD OHGO
OD OH GOD OH GOD
OHGOD OHGOD OHGO
OHGOD OHGOD OH
GOD OH GOD
WOW.

GOD. THIS DIALOGUE IS HORRIBLE.
NOT ONLY THAT, IT'S GOT NOTHING TO DO WITH RICHARD II.
YEAH. HE'S TOTALLY GOTTA RETCON THIS SHIT.
NO
THIS BULL SHIT IS BULLSHIT MAN
SHAKES HISTORY STRIKES BACK PEARE

KING JOHN

KNEEL BEFORE FRANCE
NEVER, YOU FRENCH DICKHOLE
NOW THAT KING JOHN IS PREOCCUPIED, I CAN KILL HIM AND PLACE MY SON ON THE THRONE!
HUH?
HUSH, DEAR. MOMMY'S WORKING.

SAY-Y-Y! THE FRENCH'RE GONNA KILL US BRITS, EVEN IF WE WIN!
LET'S GO BACK TO KING JOHN!
BUT HE KILLED THAT KID!
WHATEVER. HAIL KING JOHN!
WHEW! I'M GLAD MY SOMEWHAT LOYAL SUBJECTS HAVE OVERLOOKED MY ROLE IN THAT KID'S ACCIDENTAL DEATH.
OO! WINE! THANKS, DISGRUNTL'D MONK!
WHATEVER.

THE LIFE & DEATH OF RICHARD II

THANKS FOR MAKING ME KING, GUYS!
HEY EXTON, CAN YOU BRING RICHARD II HERE SO I CAN TALK TO HIM?
"KILL RICHARD IN THE FACE." GOT IT!
SLAM
ZOOM
WAIT!
I --
AH, HE'S TOO FAR.

KING HENRY IV pt. 1

FALSTAFF! YOU KILLED HOTSPUR??
HAL! WHY CAN'T YOU BE MORE LIKE FALSTAFF? OR HOTSPUR?? JESUS!
PWNED FTW
GOOD
HAL
TIME TO DRINK MY DADDY ISSUES AWAY

KING HENRY IV pt. 2

MEAN WHILE
UR MAI BFF RITE HAL
ABSOLUTELY, FALSTAFF.
PRINCE HAL! YOUR FATHER HAS PASSED. YOU ARE NOW KING!
THANK FUCK FOR THAT.
GET ME AWAY FROM THIS HUMANOID

KING HENRY V

BONJOUR, HENRI le 5eme! WE 'AVE A GEEFT POUR VOUS!
NYAH HA HAA!
WHY, THANK YOU. I -- TENNIS BALLS?!
THIS MEANS WAR

LATER IN FRANCE
WE TORE INTO THEIR BREACH AND TORE 'EM A NEW RECTUM, SIRE!
OUI, MONSIEUR! YOU 'AVE BEAT ZE CHEESE OUT OF US. TAKE MY DAUGHTER, S'IL VOUS PLAIT!
LE QUACK
I LITERALLY RULE

KING HENRY VI pt. 1

SIRE! WE'VE GOT JOAN of ARC!
où mon humeur doit-elle me guider?
BUSY.
ANYWAYS, WE BRITS THINK IT'D BE SPLENDID TO HAVE MARGARET HERE MARRY HENRY. AND I PROMISE NOT TO MANIPULATE HER TO PURSUE MY OWN ENDS.
OK
BE THE MR. BIG TO MY CARRIE

KING HENRY VI pt. 2

GLOUCESTER'S DEAD!
DAMMIT, SUFFOLK--
SUFFOLK'S DEAD TOO!
SWING
OH. WELL, TIME TO JET THEN, MAR-- --UH--
HE WAS SO MISUNDERSTOOD

KING HENRY VI pt. 3

MARGARET, I'LL SHOW YOU MERCY. I'LL LET YOU LIVE AND KILL YOUR SON INSTEAD.
THAT'S... AWESOME.
YOU WON'T BE LOVED
GAK
I AM RICHARD I AM I AM AN ISLAND
EXECUTIONER
HEY! SHOULDN'T THE SEQUEL BE EDWARD IV-- OH.
RICH 3

THE LIFE & DEATH OF RICHARD III

SO WHAT'D TRICKY DICK SAY BEFORE YOU KILLED HIM?
I DUNNO. SOMETHING ABOUT A HORSE.

KING HENRY VIII

WOLSEY, I JUST FOUND OUT THAT YOU'VE BEEN UNDERMINING MY AUTHORITY BY BEING A LIAR. LEAVE MY FACE.
I HAVE BEEN ACTING MOST UNPRIESTLIKE
Uhh... I DON'T WANNA SOUND GREEDY, BUT SINCE KATHERINE JUST DIED, CAN I TAKE HER SPOT?

OH GOD I'M A FAILURE. JUST WHAT HAVE I DONE WITH MY LIFE?! EVERY-THING I TOUCH TURNS TO GARBAGE. I'M THE KING MIDAS OF ASS.
I SHOULD' LISTENED T MY MUM A BECOME A DOCTO
JULY
DEAD LINE

MEW
IN THERE
BY
HEY WILLY! GOT AN END TO HAMLET YET?
JUST AD-LIB IT, REGGIE.
WELL, HOW DO WE END IT?
JUST KILL EVERY ONE
UHH... OKEE-DOKE.
Tragedies
(TOT)

TROILUS & CRESSIDA

OKAY.
HECTOR JUST FUCKED UP YOUR LOVER, PATROCLUS.
BRING ME HIS SCROTUM, MY ARMY OF MYRMIDONS
"DEAR T
GREECE IS AWSUM! WE'LL B FRIENZ 4VR BUT ITS OVR SORRIES LUV
C."
SORRY DUDE

CORIOLANUS

...NUS
...S A
...EBAG
YOU SUCK, CORIOLANUS!
I DIDN'T VOTE 4 'ANUS
NO! YOU SUCK, CROWD!
I'M COMIN' BACK WITH MY NEW VOLSCAN BUDS TO FUCK YOU GUYS UP!

THE FAMILY GOT ME TO THINK IT OVER, AND I THINK I WAS JUST BEING RASH. SO I'M GOING HOME..
GURK.
I THOUGHT WE WERE FRIENDS

TITUS ANDRONICUS

--WHAT THE FUCK WAS THAT??!

ROMEO & JULIET

WHOA.
COUPLES SHOULD COMMUNKATE
GASP!

TIMON OF ATHENS

I'M POOR!
FUCK YA LATER!

JULIUS CAESAR

MAN.
KILLING CAESAR WAS A BAD IDEA, DON'T YOU THINK--
OH.
WHO'S THE MAN NOW, DOG

MACBETH

I'M NOT A PUSSY ANYMORE-- GLURK--
DIE, YOU DICK

HAMLET

WHAT THE FUCK HAPPENED HERE?

KING LEAR

I LOVE YOU!
I LOVE YOU MORE!
YOU'RE OKAY, BUT I DO HAVE PROBLEMS WITH SOME THINGS TH YOU DO. SUCH
GET. OUT.

NOW THAT I'M BLIND, I CAN SEE THAT I HAVE POOR JUDGEMENT SKILLS!
WORDPLAY!
FOR SALE
#1 DAD

OTHELLO

DON'T WORRY ABOUT THE PROMOTION. AND YOUR OLD LADY IS MESSIN' AROUND.
NOT ON MY WATCH, BABY.
YOUR HUSBAND ROCKS
THANKS

I WISH I WAS MORE TRUSTING--
CROAK
EVIL WINS--
HUH?
KLAK!

ANTONY & CLEOPATRA

ROME'S SURROUNDED US AND I'VE BEEN WOUNDED! CLEO, I-- I LOVE--
GASP
THAT BITES. SPEAKING OF WHICH, WHERE'D I PUT THOSE VENOMOUS COBRAS..?

CYMBELINE

IMOGEN, MY WONDERFUL DAUGHTER, YOU ARE MY SOLE HEIR. ONCE YOU HAD 2 BROTHERS, BUT THEY ARE NO MORE.
ANYWAYS. WHAT DID YOU WANT?.
I KINDA ELOPED WITH POSTHUMOUS, INSTEAD OF MARRYING MY STEP-BROTHER CLOTEN. DAD.
IT'S GOING TO BE A HARD COMMUTE FOR YOU AFTER I'M DONE EXILING POSTHUMOUS' LECHEROUS ASS.

I, THE DOCTOR WHO WAS TO POISON THE FAIR IMOGEN, HAVE TO TELL YOU THAT 1. SHE HATED IMOGEN and 2. SHE WAS MANIPULATING CLOTEN TO GET TO THE THRONE!
HUH.
THAT'S WHY WE WERE, Y'KNOW, "DEAD."
BY THE WAY, WE'RE YOUR SONS.
YA
ALSO, SHE JUST DIED. STRESS.
HEY DAD, I GOT POSTHUMOUS A FRUIT BASKET WITH A CARD THAT SAYS, "MY BAD, WIFE IS A BITCH." HA! I GET IT!
IT'S COMPLICATED!

Biographies

Andrew Wheeler

Andrew Wheeler is a British homosexual, just like Shakespeare. He enjoys tea, warm beer and UFC, just like Shakespeare.

Brian Joseph Harvey

BFF B.A. (Hons), MLIS

Brian was born in the Free City of Danzig. After escaping the Siberian Gulag, he was raised by a family of wolves before fighting his way across Eurasia to settle in Toronto. Now he sometimes watches the TV, reads books and drinks.

Parrish Ziganian

Parrish is the many-named whiz with impecable handwriting. When not petting his many cats and girlfriend, he can be found reading and working on his various schemes. Most of which have proven fruitful.

Krystle Tabujara

Krystle Tabujara is a professional muse and international artist model...though Eric Kim has never sketched her naked (yet).

Fin